THE Emma Smith WE KNOW

A collection of memories and recipes from
Emma, as recalled by her posterity.

WRITTEN & COMPILED BY
DARCY KENNEDY &
ANGELINE KENNEDY WASHBURN

Published by
>   The Joseph Smith Jr. and Emma Hale Smith
>   Historical Society, Inc.
>   Alpine, UT

Printed in the United States of America.

ISBN 978-0-9709151-8-4

THE *Emma Smith* WE KNOW

A collection of memories and recipes from
Emma, as recalled by her posterity.

WRITTEN & COMPILED BY
DARCY KENNEDY &
ANGELINE KENNEDY WASHBURN

The Joseph Smith Jr. and Emma Hale Smith
Historical Society, Inc.
Alpine, UT

Acknowledgements

We are grateful to all of the family members who were so willing to give their thoughts and feelings as a labor of love and tribute to their great-grandmother Emma. We are thankful for the many family members and those who have loved Emma and Joseph and have preserved the precious journals and writings that made this book possible.

Many times I have taken descriptions related to Emma's cooking from accounts given by her grandchildren that were scattered among their writings and have strung them together in one paragraph. The writings of these children have been preserved by Buddy Youngreen and would have been a great loss to us all had he not made them so easily accessible by including them in his book "Reflections of Emma."

We would also like to acknowledge Gracia Jones, who has always been there for us with love, wisdom, and her vast knowledge of our family.

We are grateful to our husbands, Nathan Washburn and Mike Kennedy, who walked the floor late at night as we worked late into the night and cared for children and grandchildren and took care of household necessities. Special thanks the Washburn family for their time and support that allowed Angeline the time to work on this project. We appreciate Nathan's never-ending support of the Joseph Smith family and Mike's untiring work for the Joseph Smith family which has long been an inspiration to us all.

–Darcy Kennedy and Angeline Kennedy Washburn

Contents

Preface

Frederick Alexander Smith—*My Mother Emma's Apron*   1

Charles Edward Bidamon—*My Knowledge of Emma*   3

Emma Belle Smith Kennedy—*Grandmother's Eyes*   5

Tory Savage—*Affectionate Emma*   9

EMMA'S RAISIN COOKIES RECIPE   11

Gracia Jones—*My Great-Great Grandmother*   13

Relief Society Minutes   17

Angeline Kennedy Washburn—*I Knew Emma Was There*   21

EMMA'S PEANUT BRITTLE RECIPE   25

Robert Wendell Smith—*I Heard Emma*   27

BROWN SUGAR COOKIES RECIPE   35

Dawn A. Schmith—*She Gave Up So Much*   37

Emma & Joseph (Poem)   41

Emma Belle Smith Kennedy—*My Grandmother*   43

Darcy Kennedy—*It Takes a Tender Mother*   45

Emma Belle Smith Kennedy—*A Journal Entry*   49

FRITTERS (CANDIDATES) RECIPE   51

Kimberly Jo Smith—*Her Lovely Countenance*   53

The Willow Song (Poem)   58

Donna Smith Naegelin—*Tenacity to Survive*   59

CORN BREAD RECIPE   63

David J. Denning—*I Always Felt a Love for Emma*   65

Nancy Sue Smith—*Epitome of Motherhood*   67

EMMA'S BISCUIT RECIPE   69

Lori Kay Savage—*I Turn My Thoughts to Emma*   71

Vida E. Smith—*Our Heritage* (Poem)   73

TONICS AND HERBS RECIPE   75

Emma Hale Smith—*My Blessing* 77

David Hyrum Smith—*An Appeal to My Brother* 79

Michael A. Kennedy, Jr.—*Emma, Frightened and Alone* 81

Michael A. Kennedy, Sr.—*Choice of Joseph's Heart* 85

Lorena Normandeau—*Where Are My Children?* (Song) 87

Emma's Passing 91

Appendix

    Family Chart—Children of Joseph and Emma

    Contributors

    Notes

THE JOSEPH SMITH JR. & EMMA HALE SMITH HISTORICAL SOCIETY

All proceeds go to The Joseph Smith Jr. and Emma Hale Smith Historical Society, Inc., a non-profit organization.

www.josephsmithjr.org

Preface

In creating this book we hope to give readers an insight into the family's memories and feelings of Emma. The earliest memories of Emma evolved a lot around Emma's kitchen and, as we have witnessed, in the lives of many of her descendants they still do. By compiling recipes that have been passed down either through the family, or simply the ages, we hope you will find the warmth of Emma's love and hospitality as you try these recipes that have warmed many a kitchen. We have also tried to maintain the flavor of the original writings of the grand-children living in the 1800s and early 1900s. However, to make reading easier, we have edited some parts or made grammatical and punctuation changes for clarity.

We wanted you to be able to see the values and love Emma had for her fellow man and particularly her Relief Society sisters, as exemplified in the Relief Society minutes for meetings throughout 1842. We will never forget the joy we felt as we held them in our hands and could see Emma's concerns that have become our concerns today. She was concerned that we be ready to take care of one another, relieving the distressed, doing "good" continually, and to be honest in our dealings. She was concerned that we help each other develop high morals and to guard one another's character and reputation; she hoped this society of sisters would give relief and be a benevolent society. Her wisdom comes alive through these pages as her concerns reach past her day into our day, past her concern for only her family to concern for all families, and past her individual needs to the needs of those around her.

So much of what has been known and said of Emma has come through historical documents and perceptions that are like looking at the sun through a peep hole—it is far from the entire illumination. Through these writings we hope you will come to know better the Emma that we know.

Emma Hale Smith was born in Harmony, Pennsylvania on July 10, 1804 to Elizabeth and Isaac Hale. She met Joseph Smith Jr. while he worked for Josiah Stowell, an acquaintance of the Hale family, and boarded at the home of Emma's parents during the year of 1825. Emma's father was not in favor of their courtship or of their hopes to marry, so after their petitions for his blessing fell on deaf ears, they eloped and were married January 18, 1827.

She knew Joseph to be the Prophet of this dispensation and that he had been called to restore all things that God had ever given to man since the beginning of time. Emma's life was one that the Adversary tried to derail as she was the strength and stability Joseph needed to keep going. In their seventeen years of marriage and support of the Lord's work, she moved eleven times, and served the Lord in many capacities. In the midst of all of this, her husband was torn from her again and again for long periods of time. She also suffered the loss of six of her eleven children. By the time her husband Joseph died in June 1844, she had lost twelve family members to death in those short seventeen years of marriage.

As a family we know Joseph was guided and inspired as he lead the Church; we also know he was guided and inspired in the choice of the love of his youth, Emma.

—Darcy Kennedy and Angeline Kennedy Washburn

Family picture of all of Emma's descendants through her children Joseph III, Alexander, and David. (1915)

Emma Belle Izatt, fourth great-granddaughter of Emma, wearing a flour sack apron similar to Emma's.

My Mother Emma's Apron
Frederick Alexander Smith (1862–1954)
Emma's grandson

Frederick Alexander Smith said of Emma that she wore a small-sprigged lavender calico dress with a clean unhemmed flour sack pinned around her. In his own words he describes her as being "an exceptional and substantial cook." He remembered her cooking pastries, pies, cookies, doughnuts and chicken, and that she cooked over an open fire in the fireplace with a crane that held the covered kettle in which she would roast her meat.[1]

Pictured above is Frederick Alexander Smith holding his grandson, Charles Meridith Trumble.

Emma Smith McCallum, Emma's granddaughter, said of Emma that visitors would ask to see Grandmother. She always wore an apron and while standing and talking she would turn her apron up at the corners and finger it.[2]

Charlie Bidamon, Emma's stepson.
At the age of 64, Emma began to raise four-year-old Charlie.
She died in 1879 when Charlie was fifteen years old.
(Photo from Ruth Brown, "Reflections of Emma"
by Buddy Youngreen)

My Knowledge of Emma
Charles Edward Bidamon (1864–1944)
Emma Smith's stepson whom she took in as a young child and raised as her own.

Wilmette, Illinois
238 Catalpa Place.
August 10, 1940

Mr. L. L. Hudson
Nauvoo, Illinois.

My Dear Friend,

I was quite surprised and pleased a few days ago to receive a letter from our old pal Frederick A. Smith. It seemed a voice from out [of] the almost dead past, as it is almost 70 years since I last saw him. He said that he was writing from the Mansion House and was attending a Reunion in Nauvoo, and that he had met you and had a talk about old times, and that he would very much like to see me. [H]e said he expected to be in Chicago the latter part of August or the first of September and would look me up. I certainly should like to see him.

In his letter he asked me to make a statement of my knowledge of his grandmother Emma Smith Bidamon, as I was raised in her home, and know what kind of woman she was.

I do not think there are any living persons who knew her better than you and I, and I know that we can vouch for her kindly disposition and humane characteristics.

I should know her as I was a member of the family, and you should know her as the greater part of your boyhood days were spent at the Mansion.

I was taken into the home of Emma Smith Bidamon in 1868 at the age of four years and was as one of the family until her death in 1879.

As to my recollections of her, she was a person of very even temper. I never heard her say an unkind word, or raise her voice in anger or contention. She was loved and respected by the entire community (all who knew her) and at her funeral, which the whole countryside attended, many tears flowed showing grief at her parting.

She has a queenly bearing without the arrogance of a queen, and was a noble woman living and showing a charity for all, loved and beloved.

With best regards to all my friends and best wishes for yourself and family.

I remain as ever yours affectionately,

(Signed) Charles E. Bidamon[3]

Grandmother's Eyes
Emma Belle Smith Kennedy (1869–1960)
granddaughter of Emma Smith

When I think of the words of the Savior, "My God hast thou forsaken me," I have evidence in my mind of their meaning and significance. I can understand that, for many times I have found myself in the same situation—not in the body, but in discouragement. I have felt that way; I know what my Christ felt when he spoke that way. In burying my loved ones there were difficult things to think about, but in Mark it says that the Savior was laid in a sepulchre of stone. He was never covered with dirt. Perhaps this is not significant to many, but when I read this I think, "My father was lowered into the grave, but my Savior was put into a sepulchre."

I never knew what it was to have a grandfather. My mother's father was killed in helping a co-worker. My mother was raised by Sister Bidamon, left alone at seven years. She was one of the many of those whom Emma raised, four different girls that Emma Bidamon gave homes to. She was one of the grandest people that ever lived.

She was alone, and would share the agony of her soul with my mother, so my mother told me.

My mother was a better educated woman than Joseph was a man. Her family was better off financially than was his. Her parents were opposed to the marriage and they ran away and were married. You know how parents feel about that. Her people first turned against her and she was left alone. In later years some of her family softened according to everything that my grandmother knew. She seemed to cover them with the cloak of charity. She held no ill feelings against her people. That is another grand thing about her. How many of us could hold to ourselves all that Emma had to keep? There were times when it must have been very hard.

A Utah man came and asked me once if I knew that Joseph Smith was a drunkard. At that time all men were drinking. I know my father, David, and his brother Joseph did not drink, and I told him that I did not think their father was a drunkard. He answered, "But they had a bar in their home." This is how that was: When grandmother and grandfather were away on a visit, a good brother put a bar in the Nauvoo Mansion house. When they came home and went in, Emma stopped and said to her husband, "Either that goes out or I do." That is the only time I ever heard of this.

I was just a little girl when I left Nauvoo; I can remember a little about it, though. My little sister, Grace, had done something cute. My grandmother was laughing but her eyes were sad. I later said to my mother, "When we laughed, Grandmother laughed but not with her eyes." My mother's eyes sparkled so when she laughed. Mother's reply was, "No, your grandmother knew great tragedy." Her eyes always looked sad. She loved Joseph, her husband. You can imagine for anyone who had such a great love, such tragedy would leave a great mark. It did in her eyes.

My grandmother used to buy her materials (foods) by the barrel. My brother was two years younger than I.

We used to love to go to the garret, where brown sugar was kept in barrels. The moisture would make the sugar hard around the edges. Grandmother would break off a little for us to eat as candy. She was a very gracious woman, although at that time I did not realize how great was her dignity. When she would give us the sugar, she would smile at us.

We left Nauvoo and went to northern Missouri. There the word came that Grandmother had passed away. One day—it was tomato time—Mother took me and my brother to pick tomatoes. She was at one end of the patch and I was at the other. I saw her sitting crying. I went to her and put my arms around her, asking what was the matter. "Your grandmother is dead, and she is the only mother I ever knew," was her reply. So you can see the love she had for the woman who had raised her, and remember she was also her mother-in-law.

Grandmother was a very independent person. She married Major Bidamon for protection. He was not a godly man, but he took care of Emma and her children.

Two of her sons, Joseph and Alexander, went to see her during her last illness. Her other son was confined to the hospital for the insane at this time. Talk about tragedies: they went in and sat by her side, and then she told them where their father was buried. She had buried him with the aid of a Negro, a colored man. She explained how she had planted a lilac bush by his grave. There was a little house there where they kept the bees. In those days they thought they had to be housed in winter. She told how she had buried Joseph and planted the lilac bush at his head. The Missouri River overflowed and washed all

7

away—the house, and everything, but the little lilac bush.

She said, "Now, boys, I want you to bury me just as close to your father as you can," and they did—so near that it was only eight feet from his grave, they found in later years when they moved the bodies to their present resting place.

After she had told the story of the great tragedy and of her husband's grave, she said, "If you will turn me over, I think I will go to sleep." They gently turned her over—their mother, whom they loved so much, so burdened with the burdens of life. Then they sat back in their chairs, knowing that in a little while she would be gone.

Soon she said, "Be patient, Joseph." Joseph, her son who was sitting there, said, "I'll try, Mother." In a few seconds she said, "Now, Joseph, I will go with you." Her son, Joseph, said, "I am sure that my father came for my mother."

I am proud of what I saw at the Conference. I saw four grandsons of the martyr—Israel A. and Wallace, sons of Joseph; Frederick A., son of Alexander, and Elbert A., son of David. Emma Smith raised the three boys.

I hope that in my life I may do something that will honor that grandmother of mine. None of us could remember anything of her but love, and none of us need ever be ashamed of anything that her sons did. It is a beautiful heritage, and if I were to place a flower on any grave, I would place it on the grave of Emma Smith Bidamon.[4]

Affectionate Emma
Tory Savage
third great-grandson of Emma Smith

To me, Emma is just as the prophet Joseph Smith said she was, affectionate. As I cast my thoughts back to yesteryears I imagine a beautiful, strong woman who was ready and willing to suffer through and endure all that must needs be suffered to ensure eternity with her family.

I cannot begin to express the love and gratitude I have for the great woman Emma Smith was. She stood by her husband, the latter-day Prophet, through all trials and pit falls. She faithfully endured relentless persecution and uncertainty throughout her life and yet she stood unmoved and affixed on the right side of both her God and her eternal companion, Joseph Smith. Oh, how can I express such love and devotion I have for this stalwart saint, Emma Smith, wife of the prophet, mother of many.

When Emma's children had friends over to play, they would be afraid to go home dirty, so Emma gave them some of her own children's clothes to wear. She would then clean up their clothes and give them cookies that she always had on hand.

Tradition says the children managed to become dirty more often.

Emma's Raisin Cookies

This recipe came from Emma Hale Smith's granddaughter. Emma was famous for her good cookies. This has been a favorite recipe in our family for as long as I can remember.

Warning: this cookie is not low calorie–but it is delicious. Some like to cook them so they remain softer; my son likes his burnt. I usually do some each way. —Gracia Jones

½ cup shortening	2 cups raisins (less is optional)
¾ cup butter	2 teaspoons soda
2 cups brown sugar	½ teaspoon salt
4 eggs	1 teaspoon cinnamon
½ cup milk	1 teaspoon nutmeg
4 cups rolled oats	½ teaspoon cloves
2 cups flour	2 cups nuts (less is optional)

Mix shortening and sugar together; add eggs one at a time. Beat well. Add milk and mix well. Mix flour, salt, soda, and spices together in separate bowl, then add them all at once and mix well; add raisins and mix. Add oatmeal and mix. Let dough sit for several hours or overnight; drop with teaspoon onto lightly greased baking pan–a good tablespoonful is about right. Bake in preheated oven (375°F) for about 10 minutes (depends on your oven. Watch so they don't burn).

Remove from pan carefully, with spatula; cool on wax paper or cooling rack. When cool you can freeze or store the extra in a tight container to keep them from drying out.

Current grave site of Joseph, Emma, and Hyrum Smith.
Nauvoo, IL

My Great-Great Grandmother
Gracia Jones
second great-granddaugher of Emma Smith

Emma lived almost thirty-five years after the martyrdom of her Prophet-husband. She died on April 30, 1879 in her seventy-fifth year. In her last years she was greatly loved, and in the last hours of her life she was attended by her family: Louis Bidamon, Julia, Joseph III, and Alexander. According to Alexander, Emma seemed to sink away, but then she raised up and stretched out her hand, calling, "Joseph! Joseph!" Falling back on Alexander's arm, she clasped her hands on her bosom, and her spirit was gone. Both Alexander and Joseph thought she was calling for her son Joseph, but later, Alexander learned more about the incident.

Sister Elizabeth Revel, Emma's nurse, explained that a few days earlier Emma had told her that Joseph came to her in a vision and said, 'Emma, come with me, it is time for you to come with me.' "As Emma related it, she said, 'I put on my bonnet and my shawl and went with him; I did not think that it was anything unusual. I went with him into a mansion, and he showed me through the different apartments of that beautiful mansion.' And one room was the nursery. In that nursery was a babe in the cradle. She said, 'I knew my babe, my Don Carlos that was taken from me.' She sprang forward, caught the child up in her arms, and wept with joy over the child. When

Emma recovered herself sufficient she turned to Joseph and said, 'Joseph, where are the rest of my children?' He said to her, 'Emma, be patient and you shall have all of your children.' Then she saw standing by his side a personage of light, even the Lord Jesus Christ."

Finding this testimony reminded me how precious each soul is in the sight of our Savior, whose compassion and power to save is beyond all comprehension. All of us make mistakes and are in need of repentance. Whenever we withdraw from the fellowship of the Saints and cease to partake of the sacrament on a regular basis, we tend to lose our way and become subject to misunderstanding—especially if our course has been set by real or imagined injury to our feelings or pride. This could happen to any of us, including my dear great-great-grandmother.

As I reflect upon all I have learned from Emma's life, I feel great reverence for the testimony she has borne of the divine authenticity of the Book of Mormon and for her precious vision of Joseph and her baby. Her legacy to us in her final witness is that she and all of us, through the ordinances restored by the Prophet Joseph Smith, have the opportunity to be with our families in eternity.

I am grateful beyond measure to my great-great-grandparents, for their commitment and sacrifice to the Lord's work. I love and appreciate the missionaries who opened the way for me to gain a testimony of my Heavenly Father and his Son, Jesus Christ, for although I did not know of God, yet I had longed for knowledge of the truth all my life. I gratefully acknowledge the power of the Holy Ghost, who enlightened my mind with the testimony: "It's true! It's true!"[5]

Emma did set an example of virtue, in word and deed. All her days Emma's house was never empty, as widows and orphans, the hungry, the sick, the lame, and the weary from all walks of life found rest there. Emma nursed the sick, comforted the lonely, and even in her own poverty, she divided her meager resources with those who were in need. It was not a grim duty to her, but a matter of fact. Emma wore her calling as "first lady" with dignity. Years later a friend remembered, "Sister Emma was benevolent and hospitable; she drew around her a large circle of friends, who were like good comrades. She was motherly in her nature to young people, always had a houseful to entertain or be entertained."

Joseph described his feelings when she came to see him while he was in hiding: "How glorious were my feelings when I met the faithful and friendly band, on the night of the eleventh, on Thursday, on the island at the mouth of the slough, between Zarahemla and Nauvoo; and what unspeakable delight and what transports of joy swelled my bosom, when I took by the hand, on that night, my beloved Emma—she that was my wife, even the wife of my youth, and the choice of my heart. Many were the reverberations of my mind when I contemplated for a moment the many scenes we had been called to pass through, the fatigues and the toils, the sorrows and sufferings, and joys and consolations, from time to time, which had strewed our path and crowned our board. Oh what a commingling of thought filled my mind for the moment, again she is here, even in the seventh trouble—undaunted, firm, and unwavering—unchangeable, affectionate Emma!"[6]

Portrait of Emma Smith.
By Permission Buddy Youngreen

A Record of the Organization and Proceedings of the Female Relief Society of Nauvoo, IL

Emma Hale Smith became the first Relief Society President of The Church of Jesus Christ of Latter-day Saints on March 17, 1842.

Nauvoo Lodge Room
Relief Society Minutes
March 17th 1842

President Emma Smith remarked—We are going to do something EXTRAORDINARY—when a boat is stuck in the rapids; with a multitude of Mormons on board, we shall consider THAT a loud call for relief; we expect extraordinary occasions and pressing calls.

On what to call the Society:

President Joseph Smith said—Benevolence is a popular term and the term Relief is not known among the popular societies. Relief is more extended in its significa-tion than Benevolent and might extend to the liberation of the culprit—and might be construed by our enemies to say that the society was to relieve criminal and to relieve a murderer which would not be a benevolent act. President Emma Smith said the popularity of the word Benevolent is one great objection—no person can think of a word as associated with public institutions, without thinking of the Washingtonian Benevolent Societies which was one of the most corrupt institutions of the day—do not wish to have it called after other societies in the world. President Joseph Smith arose and said that he had no objection to the word Relief. . . .

President Emma Smith proceeded to make appropriate remarks on the subject of the Society—"its duties to others, also its relative duties to each other, viz: to seek out and relieve the distressed, that each member should be ambitious to do good—that the members should deal frankly with each other to watch over the morals—and be very careful of the character and reputation of the members of the institution.

Question: P.A. Hawkes—what shall we reply to interrogators relating to the object of this society? President Emma Smith said—"For charitable purposes."

March 24th 1842

Measures to promote union in this society must be carefully attended to—and that every member would be held in full fellowship—as a society hoped they would divest themselves of every jealousy and ill feeling toward each other if any existed, that we should bring ourselves into respectability here and everywhere else—said she rejoiced in the prospects before her—continued by saying that those wishing to join the society could have the privilege. No one need feel delicate in reference to inquires about this society; there is nothing private—its objects are purely benevolent. . . . said all proceeding that regard difficulties should be kept among the members—as to the Institution its objects are charitable—none can object to telling the good—the evil withhold—hoped all would feel themselves bound to observe this rule.

March 30th 1842

President Emma Smith said—we were going to learn new things—our way was straight—said we wanted none in this society, but those who could and would walk straight, and were determined to do good and not evil—

April 14th 1842

President Emma Smith arose and addressed the meeting by saying the disagreeable business of searching out those who were iniquitous seemed to fall on her—said it was an unpleasant task, that her desire was to do good—wished all the members of the society to assist her and it was necessary to begin at home—to eradicate all evil from our own hearts, and warn those who wish to join with us to come calculating to divest themselves of everything wrong and unite to expose iniquity, to search it out and put it away—she said the society had other duties to attend to, than seeing to the wants of the poor. Exhorted the members so to conduct as to have the honor of commencing a good work and of carrying it out—afford the necessity of walking in a manner that would be approbated of God.

May 13th 1842

Mrs. President said that this day was an evil day—that there is as much evil in this as in any other place—said she would that this society were pure before God—that she was afraid that under existing circumstances the sisters were not careful enough to expose iniquity—the time had been when charity had covered a multitude of sins—but now it is necessary that sin should be exposed—that heinous sins were among us—that much of this iniquity was practiced by some in authority, pretending to be sanctified by President Joseph Smith. Mrs. President continued by exhorting all who had erred to repent and forsake their sins—said that Satan's forces were against this church—that every saint should be at the post.

August 4th 1842

Mrs. President then proceeded to make observations respecting her visit to Quincy—that she was prospered—was cordially received by the Governor who assured us of his protection. She said we could govern this generation in one way if not another—if not by the mighty arm of power we can do it by faith and prayer. If we will try to live uprightly, said she believed we should not be driven. Mrs. President continued by saying, "God knows we have a work to do in this place—we have got to watch and be careful not to excite feelings not make enemies of one another."[7]

I Knew Emma Was There
Angeline Kennedy Washburn
fourth great-granddaughter of Emma Smith

I have been given several wonderful experiences by the Lord to get to know my fourth great-grandmother, Emma Smith.

My dad, Michael Kennedy, gave me a seventeen-foot ancestral chart. This long banner hangs in my home, covering three walls, and allows me to see all of the descendants of Joseph and Emma from 1832 to our present day. As I was studying it and looking over the chart I specifically looked at each of her children that died and how close to their birth they died. When my eyes reached Don Carlos, I realized that he was only fourteen months old when he died; my son William at that point in time was fifteen months old. It hit me like a ton of bricks! I sat and thought about my own son and what I would do if I had lost him. I couldn't imagine losing my son so young, and so perfect and sweet. Not only did Don Carlos die at fourteen months, but this was her fourth child who had died so young.

A few months ago my husband and I were looking forward to having another child. Not long after this, I found myself in the emergency room of the hospital with an ectopic pregnancy. I had to have surgery to remove the baby and part of the tube. Before going into surgery my husband gave me a blessing in which I was told this experience would help me to understand my ancestor Emma

Smith, for this was the only way I could. It took me a while to get over the feelings of loss and pain, especially when I would see and be around newly-born babies and pregnant mothers.

As time heals, I have looked back at that blessing with a deeper understanding of my great-grandmother and have been filled with love from my Heavenly Father and His wisdom in giving me these experiences. I thought about the babies Emma lost: Alvin, shortly after birth; Thadeous and Louisa (twins), also shortly after birth; Joseph Murdock Smith, almost a year; Don Carlos, fourteen months old; and then little Thomas, also shortly after birth. She carried each of these babies full term or almost full term—they took breath, and they were in her arms, and then they died. I had a hard time with the loss of a baby at eight weeks into the pregnancy; I couldn't imagine losing a baby after birth. I don't know how she got through the loss; not only did she lose her first child after birth, but her loss was multiplied by her worry for Joseph over the loss of the 116 manuscript pages.

Emma has taught me many things, and because of her I have learned that we can make it through anything that is thrown in our path. No matter what happens, I can always smile and continue with my life with a good attitude and complete love and kindness. She showed this love and care for others through all that she went through and endured. She has taught me that no matter what our trials are or what happens in this life it will eventually come to an end; we will live eternally with those we love and it will all be worth it.

I was also given the grand opportunity to be involved

in the making of the "Emma Smith—My Story" film. I was able to speak with the actors and actresses and to have a close relationship with those close to the film. The feelings on the set were of love and tenderness. I was able to attend all of the movie premieres. In each one of the premieres I knew Emma was there. At one point I felt her close to me, and I felt my family close to me. I knew she was proud of all that had been done for her name and the gathering of her children. She is an amazing and very strong woman; I only wish I had her strengths, her capacity to take each thing as it comes and to deal with it as she did. I look forward to the day that I can meet her and feel her embrace.

"When I was a kid growing up, my grandmother 'Nettie' Smith made it every Christmas. She said it was always something they did as a family tradition and it was Alexander Smith [Emma and Joseph's son] who had taught her how to make it and he picked it up watching his mother (Emma) make it over an open fire. Grandma 'Nettie's' husband, my grandfather Don Alvin Smith [Alexander's son], died when he was only thirty-three, leaving six little children under the age of ten. Alexander moved her and the children in next door and oversaw the raising of those children. That's what made it like we are a generation closer to Emma."

–Bob (Robert Wendell) Smith

Emma's Peanut Brittle

2 cups sugar
1 teaspoon butter
1 cup simple syrup (corn syrup)
Pinch of salt
1 cup water
2 teaspoons soda
1 pound of peanuts

Boil sugar, syrup, and water to soft ball stage. Add peanuts, butter, and salt. Cook syrup until golden brown, move from fire, stir in soda, and drop on a greased cookie sheet.

When making, use a heavy pot, such as cast iron. Stir with wooden spoon. Do not touch after having dropped the cooked mixture onto the cookie sheet. Pour mixture evenly over the cookie sheet and tip cookie sheet side to side to even it out further. The trick is learning to watch and recognize when it has reached golden brown. When it is over-cooked it is hard—when under-cooked, it is sticky.

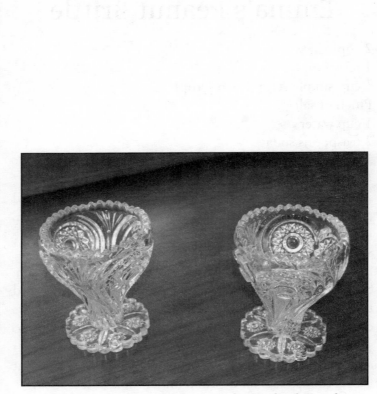

Emma's vases that once were in the Kirtland Temple

I Heard Emma
Robert Wendell Smith
second great-grandson of Emma Smith

The history of the church in my family dates back five generations. I was born in 1942 in Denison, Iowa, the youngest child of Maxwell Alexis Smith and Leone Mearle Smith. My father was Don Alvin Smith and Susan Zenetta Smith's youngest child. My grandfather was the fifth-born child of Alexander and Elizabeth Smith. My great grandfather was the third born living son of Joseph Smith, Jr. and Emma Hale Smith. Therefore, my roots go back to the beginning of The Church of Jesus Christ of Latter-day Saints.

After Joseph's death, Emma did not go to the Great Salt Lake with the caravans but stayed behind in Nauvoo and never had good contact with the Mormons again. It was shortly after this time that the Re-organized Church was founded and Emma's family and posterity were members.

I was baptized into the RLDS church in 1950 and remained a member until the mid–1960s when I became very unhappy with the church. Many years passed and during them I maintained my beliefs, which are: I believe in God, Jesus Christ his son, and the Holy Ghost as the third personage. I strongly believe that Joseph Smith had translated the book of Mormon and brought the Gospel of latter days to us.

During these years I practiced my own beliefs and

managed to break most of the Commandments and totally ignored the Word of Wisdom.

I had a great fear of the LDS church. This fear had been instilled in me by my parents as this was instilled by their parents before them. I believed my ancestry had to be kept secret or my life could be in danger as was foretold of ancestors of Joseph. Only people who were closely associated to the family knew of my ancestry, and I never talked of it until I met Dave Edwards in the early 1980s. Dave was a member of the LDS church who had been raised in the Reorganized Church. He is the only member of the LDS Church who I ever conveyed my trust in. Never once did he preach the Church to me—he knew how I felt and was a big support to my feelings.

Early in the year of 2005, I was surfing the web and ran across a site: JosephSmithJr.com. I spent several hours reading what was there. To my disbelief, everything I had been told in my early years by my dad's family lay before my eyes. There was a section that required a password to enter. So I e-mailed the site and explained who I was and what I wanted. The next day I had an e-mail to contact family president Michael Kennedy in Alpine, Utah. I immediately called him on the telephone and we talked for a long time. I found out he was the great-grandson of my grandfather's sister, and that there were many more ancestors than I knew existed.

Mike Kennedy also told me that the first Joseph Smith Jr. family reunion would be held in August of that year in Salt Lake City, and he encouraged me to attend. During the next few months I pondered in depth the idea of going but was very afraid to make the trip. I contacted my niece, Kim Larson, and asked her if she would go with me, and she said yes. The ground work was laid, but I still fought the decision to go. The day before our departure, Dave Edwards came into my office, and I told him I was not going. This was the first time he crossed me and informed me that I was going, and the next day I boarded the plane. I left Omaha, Nebraska, thinking I was a sheep being led to the slaughter. I might be going out on a nice plane, but I was coming back in a pine box.

We arrived in Salt Lake City at 12:30 p.m. and were met by John and Gwen Smith, the great-grandson of Hyrum Smith, Joseph's brother. They had been assigned to us as our host family, and we stayed in their home while we were there.

The next three days were totally packed with tours, family meetings, and banquets. There were 200 direct descendants of Joseph's and only a handful that I had ever met before. Our reception was totally awesome. The warmth shared will last a lifetime. Many of the people we came in contact with knew Joseph Smith had posterity but none had ever seen one of his descendents. The last night we went to a play at the Marriott Center on the BYU campus. When we arrived at the center we entered the room in which 23,000 people were gathered in celebration of Joseph's 200th birthday. I will never again in my life have the feeling of total emotion I felt as I stood in the middle of the stadium with my family as we received a standing ovation from 23,000 people. The program was very delightful and very well done, commemorating the entire life of Joseph. As the large voice choir sang the finale, "Praise to the Man," there was not a dry eye in the auditorium and I was totally moved with the Spirit.

That night after we returned home to John's I could not sleep. I went out to his backyard and thought of my life. I prayed for direction. I sat there in the darkness and eventually watched a beautiful sunrise. I think I knew then what I was going to do.

The next day we were guests at the performance of the Tabernacle Choir's Sunday morning program. Immediately following the program the Choir performed a special program for the Smith family, and as they sang "Joseph's First Prayer," I wept openly for the first time in 50 years. That had not happened to me before. I have never showed emotion, not even at the deaths of my parents, my wife, or my son. We bid our farewells to the family and went back to John and Gwen's and attended their Family Night with their seven children and their families.

I came home a total emotional wreck, but I knew what I needed to do.

For the next few months I did much research and soul searching to make sure that I was ready to pursue this. I also looked back to the Reorganized Church only to find out they had changed the church name, denounced the Book of Mormon, and denounced Joseph Smith as the prophet—all of which I am very opposed to. This told me the original church was the one for me to pursue.

While in Salt Lake City, I met a young man and his family: David and Rebecca Denning and their three boys, Alexander, Caleb, and Jonah. He is the son of my second cousin Gracia Jones. David is stationed here in Omaha and we have become very close. His mother was the first of the descendants to convert back to the Church, and we talked at length about it.

Early one morning a knock came to my door. When I opened it, two young men were standing there. They introduced themselves as missionaries of The Church of Jesus Christ of Latter-day Saints. They were Elder Batine and Elder Williams. I invited them in and explained to them my ancestry and what I was thinking. For the next few weeks they spent many long hours explaining the full gospel to me. I also spent several evenings in the home of David and Jodi Edwards where Elder Sandhu and Elder Johnson worked with me.

During this period many things happened that were beyond coincidence. Every time I met with missionaries I would have correspondence with one of the family members shortly after our meeting. Example one: One Wednesday afternoon Dave, Elder Johnson, Elder Sandhu, and I went to the Council Bluffs Visitors Center to watch the new movie on the life of Joseph Smith. That night when I got home, in my mail was a book entitled "Joseph and Emma." The book was from the author, my cousin Gracia Jones. (The Joseph Smith Jr. Family Organization sent this book to all of the descendants in March 2006.) Second example: One afternoon while talking with the missionaries, my cell phone rang. It was Darcy Kennedy and she said, "Hi, just felt the urge to call you, I don't know why. What are you doing?"

Through all the efforts of the Elders I had come close to making the final decision to be baptized, but one problem still stood in my way. My entire life I had questioned why Emma and her children had been left behind when the rest left for the Great Salt Lake. In my belief, she had been extremely instrumental in the Restoration. It did not make sense why she was abandoned and left to fend for herself and five children.

On a Thursday morning while driving to my place of employment, I had a life changing experience. I was listening to my radio and singing along with the gospel music group, Bill and Gloria Gaithers, when right in the middle of one of the songs my radio stopped playing. After having pounded on my dash a few minutes, I heard a woman's voice very sternly say, "Robert." There was a pause and she continued: "Follow your heart. I stayed in Nauvoo because I was tired and could travel no further." The radio started playing again as the Goodmans sang, "Joy, Joy, Wonderful Joy, Angels Are Everywhere." I was in total disbelief as to what I had heard. Had I lost my mind, or had Emma spoken to me? No matter which, the answer to my question was given and I accepted it. That Wednesday night at Dave and Jodi's I told them what had transpired. It was at Dave's with Jodi, Elder Johnson, and Elder Sandhu that I made my final decision to be baptized and I felt good about it.

While at Dave's that evening, I called Mike and Darcy to let them know my decision. Darcy instantly told me to let them know when so they could be here. I felt good as I drove home that evening. I called John and Gwen to tell them also and they said they too would be here. I could not figure the excitement that they had about my decision. I also contacted Dave and Rebecca, who also were extremely excited. We decided that May 13th would be the date so everyone who wanted to come would have time.

Several weeks before the baptism Rebecca called and asked if I would mind if her son Caleb could be baptized at the same time. This was the final touch. I was overwhelmed with emotion that the great-great grandson and the great-great-great-great grandson of Joseph were to be baptized together. This was a great honor.

Caleb and I were baptized by our cousin Michael Kennedy. The baptism talk was given by John Smith. The Holy Ghost talk was given by Dave Edwards, and then we were confirmed by Michael Kennedy. It was a very emotionally packed day. The evening was filled with close friends and loved family members. For the first time in my life I truly felt a part of the Church. We all gathered at my house after the ceremony and spent the remainder of the evening in close fellowship.

As I look back over that day, I feel the most important thing that happened was the love shared by family. Joseph and Hyrum had a love for each other that cannot be equaled again. The day Mary Fielding Smith said goodbye to Emma and her children, the two dead brother's families never reunited again until August of last year. Caleb's and my baptism was the first time that a descendant of Joseph and Hyrum worked together in the baptism of a family member. I can only imagine the rejoicing and tears that are being shed by the two brothers on the other side of the veil. Their families are once again, after 150 years, united in the love they shared for each other.

"Emma made a brown sugar cookie that is like our Ranger cookies today." —Bob Smith

Brown Sugar Cookies

1 cup butter, at room temperature
1 cup granulated sugar
1 cup brown sugar, packed
2 eggs, well beaten
2 cups sifted all-purpose flour
½ teaspoon baking powder
½ teaspoon salt
½ teaspoon baking soda
1 teaspoon vanilla extract
2 cups oats
½ cup chopped walnuts

Cream butter, granulated sugar, and brown sugar until light and fluffy. Beat in eggs, one at a time.

Sift flour with baking powder, salt, and baking soda. Stir into butter mixture. Add vanilla and nuts and stir until blended.

Drop by tablespoons onto ungreased cookie sheet. Flatten to 4-inch diameter. Bake cookies at 350°F for 10 to 12 minutes. Cookies should be slightly soft when removed from oven.

Makes 22 large cookies

Note: To be more like a Ranger cookie of today, add 2 cups of corn flakes.

Items from a 19th century kitchen.

She Gave Up So Much
Dawn A. Schmith
third great-granddaughter of Emma Smith

I was the first-born child of Thomas James Gleeson and Bonnie Irene Waters in Newcastle, New South Wales, Australia. I have a sister Glenda Mavis and a brother Tomas James (3rd).

My father was the son of Mavis Myra Wright and Thomas James Gleeson, Sr. My grandmother was the daughter of Ina Inez Smith, who was the daughter of Alexander Hale Smith, son of Joseph Smith, Jr., so Joseph Smith is my great-great-great grandfather.

My grandfather Thomas Gleeson, Sr. was Catholic, so my Grandmother became a Catholic to be able to marry in a Church as Pop would not marry outside his faith, and in those days if both people were not Catholic, they could not be married before the altar. They had to marry at the side of the church. My father and his brother Sidney were raised Catholics and both raised their children Catholics. I went to a Catholic primary school, then graduated to a Girls Catholic College for high school. I am truly grateful for the Catholic education. I was always a religious girl and was faithful to the Catholic church, attending Mass and holy days of obligation. I met my husband Dave and married him at the age of 21, and we raised our two girls, Shilo and Kim, in the Catholic faith.

When I was about 12 years of age, I can remember my mom telling me that I was a descendant of Joseph Smith. My father would never discuss it, and it was like a

37

big secret. I guess that was when I first became interested and wanted to know more. My grandmother died when I was 12, so I never got to talk to her as an adult would have. My cousin Vicki and I both feel that we were robbed of that part of our heritage when Nana died.

I can remember missionaries coming to our door, and when I told them I was a descendant, they were in disbelief that I wasn't a member of the LDS Church. One day when I visited Mom and Dad after I was married, Dad gave me a cassette that was given to him by his cousin Nancy Rogers from Toowoomba. It had Mike Kennedy, Sr. speaking on it from when he had come to Australia one time to try and connect with us Aussies. Listening to the cassette made me more curious about my family in America.

I contacted a genealogist—Janet Reakes—here in Hervey Bay who was also a member of the LDS Church, and she gave me the family organization mail address in America. I wrote to Mike and he wrote back and sent a big book of my ancestry with two missionaries. I finally had something in my hand that I could read and I was thrilled. Dad was upset with me for contacting Mike—I never knew why. Gracia and Ivor Jones also visited me here in Hervey Bay, Australia, to put family members on a big scroll.

In 2005, my cousin Vicki and I attended a combination family reunion and 200th birthday celebration of my third great-grandfather, Joseph Smith. Our main reason for attending was to correct the lack of a family book entry—our grandmother's name had been left out. I really enjoyed the reunion and couldn't get over the generosity of the LDS people; nothing was too much for them. It also became a great learning curve for me. Both Vicki and I enjoyed the reunion very much.

In 2007, I gave up trying to find the money to go to America for the reunion and sent an e-mail to my cousin Gracia to say I couldn't go due to lack of finances. Gracia sent me an e-mail back and to cut a long story short, my fare was paid for by someone in America. My trip to Nauvoo was the first time I had been out of Australia. I was so grateful for the assistance given to me to have the chance to go over. It was very educational and overwhelming, and it left a big impression on me. I came home to Australia and a month later started attending the LDS Church.

Before going to America, I was a Eucharistic Minister in the Catholic Church, very dedicated and devout. Now I am looking forward to my up-and-coming baptism into the LDS Church. It is a monstrous step for me and not without some controversy in my little family, but it is the most exciting feeling I have had in a long time.

I am already living the Word of Wisdom. I have not drunk alcohol for over 25 years. I have not smoked tobacco for 22 years and don't drink coffee or tea (tea being my last vice). Joseph sure knew what he was talking about with those substances.

I believe Joseph is a true Prophet of God, I believe he was given messages from God and that he translated the Book of Mormon from the gold plates. I believe Emma is one of the pioneers of America and Christian fellowship. The life she lived was hard with losing children, pulling up stumps, and having to go further and further away from her parents. She had no family support from her side of the family. She gave so much up to follow Joseph and help him in his mission. The saying goes, "Behind every great man is a great woman." I believe she is the great woman.

Emma & Joseph

Emma and Joseph joined as one
A gold ring bound their love
This union was a good one
It was chosen from above

Emma was Joseph's back stop
She travelled from town to town
Carrying her treasures in a wagon
Folk were mean and put them down

They lost some little babies
In times of hardship they wept
Never losing Faith in God above
Emma's safety the Lord kept

After Joseph's murder
Emma had enough
She was tired of all the running
She was tired of living rough

Emma raised her children
She cared for all her Kin
Emma did not travel to Utah
She felt the winter and its wind

The days were dark and lonely
She lived from day to day
She raised her little babies
In her own and loving way

−written by Dawn Schmith, 2008

Restored Spring House/Ice House. Nauvoo, IL.

My Grandmother
Emma Belle Smith Kennedy (1869–1960)
granddaughter of Emma Smith

Emma Smith was a lover of horses, and could handle them well.

As a child I played with her "riding habit"—it was a tight fitting jacket and long skirt, very long as in those days, ladies wore long dresses, touching the floor. Only the toe of the shoe showed. She rode a side saddle and her hat was a high crown with a shipping feather and sail. The saddle was a thing of art as it was a hand made one, beautiful. She often rode with Grandfather in great style. His horse was named "Charlie" but if I ever heard what her horse was named I have forgot.

My grandmother's door was open to all who needed protection. The boats in certain seasons went down the river to the larger cities below Nauvoo and often when gay parties came back, they would bring colored boys or girls, to dance or sing. They could not take them farther north than Quincy, IL, by law, so as Nauvoo was so close to the colored line they would drop the colored people off. On one such a trip they brought a little colored lad about 3 years old. As Grandmother's house was a hotel on the river, she got the left overs many times. Now what she did with such I never heard. I suppose there are ways of putting them by on the next boat going down, unless it was the last one of the season. Then, there must have been ways to handle it. This little one was the one of which my mother talked, of his funny little ways and his black skin but what became of him I never learned. Then when I came here to live, I learned this story. Joseph, my grandfather, saw a master flaying a small colored lad and protested. When the slave owner said, "the only way you can stop me is buy the n——," kind Joseph did. But then I learned the colored children that came into the family was as one skin—no difference was made because their skin was black.

One of them grew up with them. He was Mose. He and Grandmother, and Uncle J [Joseph III], a boy of 11 years, buried Joseph and Hyrum in the little cellar under the little brick house at the old homestead after the mob killed them—that in itself is a dark terrible story. He was a very large man and Emma told him what she wanted him to do. It was up to her to care for the bodies. She could trust no man of her own race, so with natural fear the colored man had of death, and knowing her, he knew he had to do what she said and keep it. Now the cellar was 8 x 10 [feet]. The men were over 6 feet tall, weighing over 200 pounds. He or they carried them [the bodies] across the street [about 100 feet], rolled in a blanket, and put them where she said. It was a very dark night. So Joseph III carried the lantern (a lad of 11) as they replaced the brick floor and potatoes and started across the street. The rain came, removing all trace of what their work had made on the grass around the little house. Then Emma planted the lilac bush at the corner of the little house that held all she had left of him, her lover. And it kept it well.[8]

It Takes a Tender Mother to Have a Tender Son

Darcy Kennedy
wife of Michael Kennedy, Sr.

Joseph was in the company of Benjamin F. Johnson in the dining room of the Mansion House. They were speaking in private when two of Emma's children came to Joseph. They had just left their mother and as Benjamin describes they were "all so nice, bright and sweet." Joseph pointed them out to Benjamin and said, "Benjamin, look at these children. How could I help loving their mother? If necessary, I would go to hell for such a woman."

King Lemuel, of the same mind, said in Proverbs 31:10, "Who can find a virtuous woman? For her price is far above rubies." This virtue, love and kindness are passed from parent to child down to the next generation to receptive children just like the native language spoken by the parent is also passed down. In a day of the acceptability of men being hard and tough, Emma's sons Alexander and Joseph stand out. Through their actions one can see Emma's tender ways and loving teachings being passed to the next generation, her grandchildren.

Emma's granddaughter Vida tells of a time when she was recovering from a long and aggravating illness. Her parents, Emma's son Alexander and Lizzie, whom

Emma had raised as her own, were caring for their first-born daughter. They questioned Vida to find something she would eat. Vida says, "I suddenly announced that there was one thing I wanted to eat—it was bacon." The very busy Alexander crossed the meadow and hillside to their neighbors, the Brooks, to find her a dinner of farm bacon. They were out of bacon as were all of the other neighbors. Alexander came back home and hitched up the horses Doll and Nell to ride to Sedgwick (Lamoni) to find some bacon for his sick little girl. There was none to be found, so he traveled to Eagleville, eight miles away. He returned at moonlight, bringing home a bundle of bacon. He sliced the bacon and helped to fry it up crisp and brown to feed this little daughter who said, "It tasted just right, and set the pace for other relished meals, unheeded for six months previous."[9]

Gentleness is further exemplified as Alexander gently worked side by side with his daughter Emma Belle while planting corn. As the earth was moved to the side, creating a hole just deep enough for the seeds, he would tell her to place three seeds in each of the earthen pockets they had created, saying, "One for the birds, one for the field mice, and one for me."

A few little girls who were older than eight years old and Emma Belle were playing in the Mansion House yard. They were talking about their grandfathers. Emma Belle had never heard of a grandpa so she asked where hers was and one of the older girls said, "Your grandpa was a bad man and somebody killed him." Emma Belle said, "I remember standing [and] looking at that girl and saw her look at the other and laugh. I turned, and running to the house, my father opened the door for me. I rushed in and said, 'where is my grandpa? Why can't I have a grandpa like the other girl? Was he a bad man and did men kill him and why?' But Dada [Alexander] picked me in his arm and walked over and sits down then said, 'Your grandpa was my father but he was <u>not</u> a bad man. And they killed your grandpa and my father.' His tears fell on my face. It could not have been grief for that father so long dead, but for the little girl."

Emma Belle remembers her tender Uncle Joseph III who was blind in his later years. As she neared where he was sitting outside, he said to her, "Oh Emma, I saw the young calf on the lawn and the green grass. So you see I'm not entirely shut out of sunshine and the beauties of this world yet." Emma Belle said, "I dropped in the rocker and then he put his hand on mine. My tears fell on it. How quick he turned taking my face in his hand and then said, 'don't weep my dear child . . .' Oh Uncle why does it have to be you?" Joseph Smith III replied, "Better be me than you. My life is far spent and you are here for long years yet." This kind of tenderness is a crown upon Emma's head.[10]

Photo of Emma Belle Smith Kennedy's journal

A Journal Entry
Emma Belle Smith Kennedy (1869–1960)
granddaughter of Emma Smith

I have heard people say, I wish I could have known Emma Smith, Joseph Smith's wife. I was only a little girl, as I was born in 1869 and she died in 1879, so my memory is that of a little one. She was always neat with her hair nice and smooth and so brown. I have seen her sit in her low rocker, take down her hair and brush or comb it, part it in the middle . . . then comb each side carefully till all was smooth, then bring it down over her ears and roll it in with the back hair then put her comb on each side.

Her eyes were brown and sad. She would smile with her lips but to me, as small as I was, I never saw the brown eyes smile. I asked my mother one day, "Why doesn't Grandma laugh with her eyes like you do?" and my mother said, "Because she has a deep sorrow in her heart." When we left Nauvoo for Northern Missouri, we went by boat and when on the boat we went by the Nauvoo House. There was Grandma at the window waving a table cloth and as long we could see her she waved to us a farewell. Mother said, "Watch, children, for we'll never see her again." Poor Mother wept so she could not show it to Grandma. That noble woman was all a mother could have been. As I grew older I remembered the many times I and my brother Don used to run down from the Mansion House to eat breakfast with Grandma and go with her on trips over to the house to see that everything was okay. They are sweet dreams of childhood. As I never knew a grandfather's love, one of the few things my memory holds is this incident.[11]

49

Items one would find in Emma's kitchen.

Fritters (Candidates) Recipe

Emma's grandson Frederick Alexander Smith said the candidates were served with honey or syrup. "During big political campaigns several candidates came to the Mansion House hotel for dinner and Grandmother made fritters, at the meal served with honey or syrup. Delighted—politicians asked, 'What do you call these things?' She said, 'It all depends. A year like this we call them Candidates—all puffed up and air in them.'"[12]

"Once in [the Prophet] Joseph's time, when a number of candidates and politicians came to her house for dinner and not having been notified of their coming, [Emma] made a hasty desert of a sort of fritter fried in fat. They were a hollow ball of pastry served with sauce or cream and sugar. One of the guests complimented her and asked what she called them. She smiled and answered soberly that they were called 'candidates.'"[13]

1 ½ cups flour	⅓ cup milk
1 teaspoon baking powder	2 eggs, separated
2 tablespoons sugar	Cooking oil
½ teaspoon salt	

Sift flour, baking powder, sugar and salt together. Make a well in center of dry ingredients and pour in milk. Add lightly beaten egg yolks. Blend together till batter is smooth. Fold in stiffly beaten egg whites. Chill for 30 minutes.

Form into fritters by making balls with 2 spoons dipped into hot water. Deep-fry in oil until golden brown.

"The willow tree weeps as it sways," from The Willow Song by Kimberly Jo Smith.

Her Lovely Countenance
Kimberly Jo Smith
second great-granddaughter of Emma Smith

I was twelve years old when I first saw her face, yet I did not know her name or her connection to me. Her lovely countenance, surrounded by a cascade of long, dark curls, gazed out from a small framed portrait that belonged to my Grandmother Smith. Her companion was likewise framed, settled neatly beside her there on the wall; a young man with eyes of brilliant blue, his face calm and gentle like a soft mist that falls in the early morning air, seeping into your soul. Somehow these two individuals seemed important to me, and I was moved to tears for reasons I could not understand at such a young age. I ran to ask my grandmother who they were and she replied, "Those are your great-great-grandparents, Joseph and Emma Smith."

Upon hearing of my relation to these two individuals I became anxious to know more about them. Those desires would be met with harsh and bitter words at times from some of my father's family. It was clear to me that speaking of Joseph Smith did nothing but cause discussions that eventually led to argumentative debates about a past I knew nothing about. Contentious situations always made me nervous, so I chose to pull away from any research concerning my ancestors. Throughout my childhood the only thing I knew of Joseph Smith was what I had heard from my family; that he was a fallen prophet and it was a topic not to be discussed. I knew absolutely nothing about Emma Hale Smith, yet something very dear happened that day when I saw the portraits; my heart was opened, allowing Joseph and Emma to become a part of my life. For the next twenty-four years I would walk through thorny paths surrounded by walls that had been built for generations. Somewhere along the way I learned to listen to the voices of my ancestors instead of the voice of man, eventually leading me to a place called Nauvoo.

In 1989 when my son, Bryan, was three years old, we traveled to Nauvoo, Illinois. I had read about it in a book that I had borrowed from a friend and wondered why I had never learned of it before. I was very drawn to go there, unable to deny the powerful feelings that accompanied the desire to see a place that I knew very little about. The first thing that caught my eye as we headed toward the Smith homes in Nauvoo was a large weeping willow tree located behind the Riverside Mansion. I was immediately drawn to it and felt as if I had seen it before. It seems odd to say that a tree seemed familiar to me, but that is how it felt and at that time in my life I did not know how to reason many of the things that I had experienced from my youth throughout adulthood. As we walked, I kept looking for the grave marker that had been Emma's. I saw her grave in a picture with my very young grandfather sitting on top of it. But upon entrance to the cemetery I noticed that there was one huge stone that encased three graves, the top of the stone angled upwards as if it were reclined halfway back—resting, yet keeping an eye on the goings-on around them. Beneath this stone monument lie Hyrum, Joseph and Emma Smith. Still ignorant of the bond that these three individuals shared and the depth of their history, I became curious as to why they were laying side by side. At the same time something inside of me ached, for there before me were three of my family, united in rest, and I sorrowed that so many of my family who were alive remained divided. While a young guide spoke about the sites, my eyes fell on the Riverside Mansion, or more commonly known as the Nauvoo House. It felt very dear to me, and I pictured in my mind a woman standing out on the porch facing the river as she shook her rugs clean. I was washed over by so many feelings. I yearned to know of my heritage, yet I did not know where to turn for more knowledge.

Nine years after the first of many visits that I would make to Nauvoo, I met and became good friends with Merrill Osmond. Through him I learned more about The Church of Jesus Christ of Latter-day Saints, something I had been raised to fear. Over the process of the next few years I would have a world of knowledge opened up to me about my ancestors. I finally came to know the people behind so many feelings and emotions that had coursed through my life.

On June 7, 1998, Merrill Osmond baptized me in Ava, Missouri. That special day would mark the turning point in my life in which I endeavored to learn even more about my family history. Soon after my baptism I met Gracia and Ivor Jones. Gracia is my second cousin and a dear friend. It is through her that I found many avenues to learn more about my heritage, especially about Emma.

After I came to learn more of Emma's life, the

visits to Nauvoo became more and more precious. One in particular stands out in my mind.

The day of my son's endowment in 2005, shortly before his mission, had been quite a spiritual time for us. Bryan would be the first of Joseph and Emma's descendants to go through the endowment in the Nauvoo Temple, and he had baptized my sister earlier that day. The next morning a friend had asked me to come with her to the willow tree behind the Nauvoo House. As I approached the tree I began to feel a sense of sadness and a flood of tears washed over my cheeks. While I wondered about the feelings which had rushed forward with so much emotion, a voice whispered to my heart, and I was given to know that Emma had spent much time by that tree in sorrow. I knew that what I had experienced was very real and it opened up to my heart some of the emotions that must have passed through this noble woman's life. However, I was somewhat bewildered because a willow tree usually does not live beyond one hundred years. For this tree to have seen the events that happened surrounding Joseph's death and the time after, it would have to be at least 121 years old. I would not have to wonder long about the miraculous tree. Later in the day we were touring the Community of Christ visitor's center and there found a painting by David Hyrum Smith, the last child born to Joseph and Emma. The work of art depicted the peninsula upon which the Nauvoo House and Homestead sit, and it was painted from the vantage point of a place now called David's Chamber, named for the sweet and gentle artist who favored the scenic spot on the river as a place to contemplate, write, and paint. In the painting, not far behind the Nauvoo House, we saw a young willow tree. I could not help the tears that fell down my cheeks, for the painting was dated 1860—so it is entirely possible that it was on the property in 1844. However, we knew for certain that it was indeed there in 1860.

Four months after these events I was caught up in the daily tasks of domesticity, doing dishes as I gazed periodically out the window. It was mid-morning and the sun was just breaking through the clouds. As I hummed a little tune, the words "how many tears did she cry as the willow tree swayed," came to my mind. I knew I was about to write something, so I grabbed a pen and pad and wrote a song about Emma. With every line I could feel her spirit, and that whole day was filled with inspiration as I penned seven more songs before night fell. The Willow Song has become a tribute to my great-great-grandmother in honor of the truly noble and virtuous woman that she was and still is to so many.

Getting to know Emma has given me a broader understanding of our family; she has become a true example of strength, endurance, joy and compassion. Having her in my heart has enabled me to weather many storms with an understanding and reasoning that I did not have before. More importantly, I have learned through my grandmother Emma that a united family is one of the most important things that we as a human race should focus on.

The Willow Song

Nigh on to dusk
Not a soul stirring
There's still a furrowed brow
there
Surrounded by dark aging hair
Wind whispers soft
as night trickles in
Her brown eyes remember him
The blue eyes that gazed into
hers
Once on a calm afternoon
as the trees moved in time
He held her heart
like a song that turns love into
rhyme
Hoping for peace by a spry
willow tree
She was well loved
though some judged her wrong
Not many knew how she cried
All of her life she'd been tried
Her faith was strong
as she raised her family
doing the best she knew how
All by the sweat of her brow
How many friends left their
tracks
While her family stayed

How many tears did she cry
as the willow tree swayed
Time broke her heart by the
sad willow tree
Emma at rest
as her children waited
hoping to see her once more
before she passed through the
veil's door
She lay asleep
deep in a memory
her husband Joseph was near
A time that was precious and
dear
He took her hand
and they went to a mansion
so fair
All of the children they lost
waited happily there
She said goodbye to the sad
willow tree
How many years will go by
while their family strays
Until they all learn why the
willow tree weeps as it sways
Time passes on by the sad
willow tree.

—written by Kimberly Jo Smith

Tenacity to Survive
Donna Smith Naegelin
second great-granddaughter of Emma Smith

 I was honored to be asked to write down some thoughts about Emma Smith and what she means to me. Frankly, without Emma and her strong spirit and tenacity to survive, I would not be here today. I don't know where to start, for you see, Emma Smith is my great-great-grandmother. I cannot remember a day in my life not knowing about her; however, more than once I was amazed that others knew her as well. The more I read of Emma and the better acquainted I become with my cousins, the more I recognize what an impact she has had on the family and the succeeding generations.

My great-grandfather Joseph Smith III was the eldest surviving son of Joseph and Emma's marriage. My grandfather Israel Alexander Smith was born of the union between Joseph III and Bertha Madison. Two sons were born to Israel and his wife Nina Marie Grenawalt, Joseph Perrine and Donald Carlos (my father); however, Joseph Perrine died at age 22 from pneumonia. When Joseph III left Lamoni, Iowa, he moved to a home in Independence, Missouri, where he spent the remainder of his life. This is noteworthy as this home has remained in the family and is where I live today. I have a photograph of Joseph III holding his grandson Joseph while sitting on the front porch of my house.

To imagine that Emma Smith was actually known by people whom I have known in my lifetime—what a connection! At these times I wish I could have been old enough to ask just one hour worth of questions. My grandfather was born in 1876, and I can easily imagine how Emma might have played or soothed him in the remaining years of her life. My grandfather [Israel] was such a sweet and gentle spirit that I believe reflects the love that he had been shown. I remember him singing and holding my brothers and myself, talking to us, bringing us presents from his many travels, but most of all making us feel secure and loved. I believe these attributes came from Emma. She endured so much but throughout she managed to keep her family together, and what a tight knit family it was at one time. Emma's children remained loyal to her. I have always found it interesting that for the most part the Smith men tend to be drawn to and marry strong willed women and the female descendants are themselves very strong women. In the old days I suppose it would be termed "hardy stock."

We were instilled with the need to be good to all we should meet, helping the ones in need even if it means going without ourselves, and always offering a bed or place for someone in need of rest. My father told many stories of people spending time with his family as he grew up. After reading more about Emma, I see her influence continues to reach throughout each generation. On one of the tours at Liberty Jail, the tour guide mentioned the time when Emma was living in Far West, Missouri, while Joseph was in the Liberty Jail. Alone, raising her children, a church growing ever larger with each passing day, meeting prejudice and discrimination at each corner, she remained steady in her faith; and although she had visitors when food was growing scarce, she managed to prepare a meal of cornbread and sorghum. What an example she has set! So often I have had to reach into my "inner" Emma for just one more ounce of strength, or I have told myself that my problems are trivial in comparison to what she underwent. I have been blessed.

Humor played a big role in the Smith side of the family. A long-forgotten memory was regained while I recently watched the Emma Smith movie. In the movie Joseph was singing the children's nursery rhyme "Pop Goes the Weasel" and a fond memory washed over me as I remembered how my grandfather and, later, my father sang this song to my brother Israel and me all the time. My father either sang us to sleep or read to us most nights. No doubt this was behavior learned from his own father, and I believe back to the times of Joseph and Emma.

Last night I was thinking of Emma's life and the thought came that our family has had to defend our ancestors throughout our entire lives. For some reason, complete strangers feel the need to tell us their negative feelings of Joseph and Emma, and most of the time they have no idea that we're related to them. I have had friends tell me the most absurd things, and more than once I have wondered what compels people to tell such vehement lies. With knowledge comes the peace that their misunderstandings can be easily assuaged with the truth—the truth that Joseph Smith is indeed a Prophet of God and that Emma Smith instilled in her family a love of peace, compassion and a thirst for knowledge. What a powerful couple these two were, and I believe that had I not been related to them, I would have felt myself lucky to be one of their friends.

In closing, I ask that you take a step back and look upon Emma's life in a favorable fashion. In doing so, I know that each of you will know Emma Smith to be a wonderful wife and companion to Joseph; a loyal and loving mother to her children and an inspiration to others. For indeed she was faithful!

Corn Bread Recipe

"Emma served many people and was always polite. When there was company and they didn't have anything to serve, she would make corn bread and serve it with Sorghum Syrup." –Donna Smith Naegelin

1½ cups cornmeal
½ cup flour
2 teaspoons baking powder
1 teaspoon sugar
1 teaspoon salt
¼ teaspoon baking soda
¼ cup bacon grease (¼ cup shortening or 2 tablespoons vegetable oil)
1½ cups buttermilk
2 eggs

Preheat oven to 425°F. Combine cornmeal, flour, baking powder, sugar, salt, and baking soda in large mixing bowl. Add ¼ cup grease, buttermilk, and eggs, stirring with a wooden spoon until just mixed.

In a medium-sized cast-iron skillet (or one with an oven-proof handle), add 1 to 2 tablespoons grease and heat until hot. Quickly pour the batter into the hot skillet. Place skillet into the oven and bake for 20 to 25 minutes. It is done when it is golden brown and the center springs back when lightly pressed. Best served warm and with sorghum syrup. (Sorghum is produced from the cereal grain sorghum. Sorghum can be found in health food stores and on the internet.) Feeds 8.

19th century Buttermilk pitcher.

I Always Felt a Love for Emma
David J. Denning
third great-grandson of Emma Smith

I am David Joseph Denning. I was born in 1972 at the end of the first Joseph Smith Senior Family reunion. As my mom, Gracia Jones, often said, it was amongst many of the Smith family that I came into the world.

Years passed with my presence at early Smith family reunions. I was also present at almost every fireside and talk my mother gave. I always heard of her account of learning of her heritage, and how her feelings were always led to Emma's story. I was there when my mom wrote the first book "Emma's Glory and Sacrifice." I felt and experienced every up and down with my mom during that time—the good times, the spiritual times, and the trying times. After a time we all learned that being part of this family is a joy and wonder, though it comes with its challenges and trials.

I always felt a love for Emma and admiration for her. In the summer of 1992, during my mission, my mother's *Ensign* article came out on Emma. I was so impressed with it that I translated it for many of the church members in Taiwan. It helped them learn more about our family through Emma's experiences, something they had never really heard of. All they had been taught was about Joseph being a prophet of God, translating the Book of Mormon, and then establishing the Church. I felt a great need to share what I did with the members there. I can almost say I felt the spirit of Emma there helping me as I shared in the Chinese language stories of her life and sacrifices.

I have always felt a great need when sharing my relationship to Joseph that I include her as well to help people understand that in that time there were the two of them. Both needed the other to accomplish and endure what they were called upon to experience. In so many ways I feel a great kinship to Emma, in how she stood her ground and stayed when all others left. Often I find my own opinions and views putting me at odds with others. Even though in some aspects they may be right, I tend to make up my mind and stick with it. I think this stubbornness is something that I have inherited from Emma, and I am proud of it.

I am honored to be who I am, very honored to be of the lineage I am. I love my family and feel the great need to be close and in touch with them as much as possible. May God grant us [her children] the strength to endure and the ability to accomplish what we must for our family, so Emma can have all her children.

Epitome of Motherhood
Nancy Sue Smith
second great-granddaughter of Emma Smith

My girls Heather, Shannon and I talked and came up with words we felt best described Emma Smith to us.

Emma Smith was—

> Forthright
> Dependable
> Loyal
> Giving
> Strong
> Supportive

Emma Smith was the epitome of Motherhood!

Nauvoo Mansion House where Emma served many guests.
Photo courtesy of Kenneth Mays.

Emma's Biscuit Recipe

"My mother, Mary Lorene Smith, said that when Emma ran the Mansion House, these are the biscuits she made. This recipe came from Mary Lorene Smith's recipe box!" —Nancy Sue Smith

2 cups flour   1 teaspoon salt
2 teaspoons baking powder   ¾ cup buttermilk
2 tablespoons bacon grease (shortening)

Sift the flour, baking powder, and salt together. Add the bacon grease (or shortening). Pick up flour and grease in one hand and rub back and forth with top hand two to three times and drop into the bowl. Scoop up more flour and grease and repeat the process until all resembles coarse cornmeal. (Cut in with two knives or pastry blender.) Add buttermilk and mix lightly.

Turn out on floured board. Pat out ½ to ¾ inch thick. Cut into biscuits, place on a well-greased pan, and bake until golden brown. (425°F)

Variations: Add cubed or grated cheese or raisins, cinnamon, and honey, or chopped dates and/or nuts.

Wooden biscuit cutter, as used in Emma's kitchen.

I Turn My Thoughts to Emma
Lori Kay Savage
third great-granddaughter of Emma Smith

 I have often felt very small and unimportant in the whole picture of my life, but when I feel that way, I turn my thoughts to my third great-grandmother, Emma Smith, to lift me up. Her strength and perseverance have always amazed me and given me a great deal of comfort at times when I just didn't know how I was going to make it through a difficult time. She is such an example to me of living by faith, and I am so grateful to her for that example. In 2007, I was privileged to be able to cook for our Smith family in the Nauvoo House in the same kitchen where she cooked. It was a special experience, and I felt of her love and devotion to her family.

Vida E. Smith, granddaughter of Emma Smith

"Emma instilled within the hearts of her children and grandchildren a deep and abiding tradition of caring for and nurturing those in need. This poem, written by a granddaughter, Vida E. Smith, daughter of Alexander Hale Smith, expresses an almost universal trait found within the family to the latest generation."
                                                    —Gracia Jones

Our Heritage
Vida E. Smith (1865–1945)

Like bands of gold the race to hold
Are the ties of family;
And to loved who breathe, the blessed ones leave
Some treasured legacy;
No palace grand nor wide-stretched land
Is the heritage we claim;
No gleam of gold, nor silver old,
Nor a laurel wreath of fame.

Not the heritage of some great sage
Whose name men love to tell—
Ours to spread with grace 'mid the human race
What our fathers loved so well.
Where the weak shall need we have voice to plead,
And give hope when skies bend low;
Where is sad distress reach a hand to bless,
And a son as we forward go.

While the waters run 'neath earth's great sun,
Ours to tell the way to find
Sweet psalms, oh ear, that vibrate near,
And glorious sights, oh blind!
There's a balm of rest, oh troubled breast,
And a work, oh restless hand!
Our heritage gleams in facts and dreams
And reaches to every land.[14]

*According to Emma Josepha Smith McCallum,
everything grew for Emma: potatoes, onions, turnips,
cabbage. She would pick the grapes, dip them in wax,
and hang them in the cellar in a cool place, and then
have grapes nearly all winter.*[15]

Tonics and Herbs Recipe

Everyone knew of Emma's salves and tonics.

When making this tonic, mix equal parts of catnip tea and saffron.

This was used for Scarlet Fever and Small Pox.

"Gather lots of mints, mullein stalk and sweet (roots) lobelia in garden. Sage tea—thyme sassafras bark to use—wild cherries bark—Ginseng used to be used a good deal—use Camphor on things like that (cuts)." —Frederick Alexander Smith[16]

"In the fall have a whole string of different herbs tied up to dry and cure. Make a salve—Everybody knew of Mother Bidamon's [Emma Smith] salves for cuts—bruises—fever—rheumatism—for every kind of ache and pain. Tonic made of herbs Saffron— Spearmint, Catnip." —Emma Smith McCallum[17]

*Emma Josepha Smith McCallum
(granddaughter of Emma Smith)*

First edition hymn book. Photo courtesy Kenneth Mays.

My Blessing
Emma Hale Smith (1804–1879)

These desires of my heart were called forth by Joseph sending me word . . . that he had not time to write as he would like, but I could write out the best blessing I could think of and he would sign the same on his return.

First of all that I would crave as the richest of heaven's blessings would be wisdom from my Heavenly Father bestowed daily, so that whatever I might do or say, I would not look back at the close of the day with regret, nor neglect the performance of any act that would bring a blessing. I desire the spirit of God to know and understand myself that I might be able to overcome whatever of Tradition or nature that would not tend to my exaltation in the eternal worlds. I desire a fruitful, active mind, that I may be able to comprehend the designs of God, when revealed through His Servants without doubting. I desire the spirit of discernment, which is one of the promised blessings of the Holy Ghost.

I particularly desire wisdom to bring up all the children that are, or may be committed to my charge, in such a manner that they will be useful ornaments in the Kingdom of God, and in a coming day arise up and call me blessed.

I desire prudence that I may not through ambition abuse my body and cause it to become prematurely old and care-worn, but that I may wear a cheerful countenance, live to perform all the work I covenanted to perform in the spirit-world and be a blessing to all who may in any wise need aught at my hands.

I desire with all my heart to honor and respect my husband as my head, to ever live in his confidence and by acting in unison with him retain the place which God has given me by his side. I desire to see that I may rejoice with them in the blessings which God has in store for all who are willing to be obedient to His requirements.

Finally, I desire that whatever may be my lot through life I may be enabled to acknowledge the hand of God in all things.[18]

Joseph was taken to Carthage; the blessing was never signed.

Katherine Nelson as Emma Smith on the set of "Emma Smith—My Story."

An Appeal to My Brother Frederick on His Sick Bed

David Hyrum Smith (1844–1904)

son of Emma

> Remember Brother dost thou not
> What Mother used to say?
> Remember how she taught us five
> In faithfulness to pray?
> O! shall we stand above her grave
> And in our conscience say
> That on life's road we have not walked
> As Mother showed the way?[19]

Through David's poem we see Emma's teachings to her sons. David had written this poem to his Brother Frederick who was very ill. Frederick had not shown any interest in religion. In February 1863, David wrote this to encourage his dear brother to consider and to think upon these things.

David Hyrum Smith was born November 18, 1844, after the martyrdom of his father, Joseph.

Pitcher as was used in the filming of "Emma Smith–My Story."

Emma, Frightened and Alone
Michael A. Kennedy, Jr.
fourth great-grandson of Emma Smith

In my mind, Emma Smith, the Prophet Joseph Smith's wife, was a lot like my wife in the sense that she must have got cold on cold nights, and she must have been lonely and frightened of night-time noises while her husband was away. I travel for my work and am sometimes away from home three or four days in another state. When I'm away, my wife, Meagan, calls me at night, before she goes to sleep, for comfort and a sense of safety. Sometimes she tells me that she thought she heard a noise outside and how frightening it was; but after we have talked, all is well. Emma must have gone through many frightening nights at home alone with her children, but she could not call her husband to ease her fright.

It seems to me Emma must have stood out like the North Star to other women who knew her, for she had strength and courage, whatever she was up against. As frightened and cold as she was those many nights alone, she was strong and taught her children to be brave even though the mob lurked in the darkness. Emma probably spent many times with tears, like anyone would alone; but on her knees she prayed for strength, and strength was given.

I can imagine how it was for her, with all of her young ones, especially while nursing; she had to get up many times at night to feed her baby, or to comfort a child with a bad fever, or just with a nightmare. I know the strength it takes for my wife caring for just one child at night and how tired she is the next day. I can't imagine in those times and conditions, with Joseph away for many months, in prison on false charges, especially in mid-winter, how little sleep she got taking care of her children. You can see Emma's strength in all she did; but also consider the added burden she had of her family, neighbors, and associates, saying unkind things about her husband. Her own father would tell her that she was foolish for believing Joseph's words; it was implied to her that bad things happened to her because she followed him. They would say, "How can you believe these things? Look what's happening to your family; it is of the devil."

Emma could have taken the easy way out and left Joseph and the Church. Many women in this day might have done that. But Emma had faith in Joseph, and a testimony of her Savior, Jesus Christ. She knew that her husband had been called of God to be His Prophet, to teach the restored truths of the gospel. She had a testimony that her husband saw God the Father, who introduced his Son, Jesus Christ, the Savior of the world. Emma did not see these things. She did not have an angel tell them to her. Her husband told them to her, and the Holy Ghost bore witness to her soul that what he said was true. To her it was just as good as seeing it with her own eyes. She stood side by side with her husband, through the opposition of the world and the apostasy of close friends who had also received great witnesses through the Holy Ghost, but they denied the faith when things got tough. Emma never denied the faith.

Joseph probably tried to prepare Emma many times before he went to Carthage, where he knew he would probably meet his death, but I don't think there is any way to prepare someone to lose what they hold dearest. Some may say that Emma was weak for not going out West or for other things. But I feel that if she had been asked to go with Joseph to die by his side or deny the gospel, she would have stood by her husband in faith of the restored gospel. I think that for Emma, this was not about religion—religion is what the world likes to call worship of God—but this was about Truth and Light that was coming down from heaven through her husband by direct revelation, given by the Lord Jesus Christ Himself. She knew the heavens were opened to Joseph, and that Joseph spoke many times to the resurrected Savior. She bore witness that the Savior taught Joseph how to organize His church and commissioned him to establish the priesthood again on the earth. Joseph was later murdered in cold blood, sealing his testimony with his own blood; the truths given to him, by the risen Savior, have been restored and are never to be taken again from the earth.

After Joseph did his work on the earth and was killed, Emma was left alone. It was no longer Emma's obligation to hold up the prophet of God and fight the waves of the world. Joseph's testimony was already given and sealed on the earth; the Church had been restored, the gospel planted. Emma's work—her purpose here on earth, to give strength to her husband, who was a prophet, just like Moses of old—was finished. Her greatest calling fulfilled, the giant waves came against them; instead of running away, she braced for them, hand in hand, with her husband. I know Emma kept Joseph afloat many times while he was in the depths of despair.

I love Emma for all that she stood for; for never settling for less and being an example through the calling which Heavenly Father called her to in this life, in upholding His servant, her husband the Prophet Joseph Smith. They are my fourth great-grandparents and I am proud of my heritage. I hope I can follow both their examples in following the gospel because it is full of Truth and Light for anyone seeking Christ's church. As Christ told Joseph in revelation, in the Doctrine and Covenants 1:30, He (Christ the Savior) had given them His commandments so that they could lay the foundation of the Church, "to bring it forth out of obscurity and out of darkness, the only true and living church upon the face of the whole earth, with which I, the Lord, am well pleased, speaking unto the church collectively and not individually."

Choice of Joseph's Heart
Michael A. Kennedy, Sr.
third great-grandson of Emma Smith

It has been said Joseph Smith "has done more, save Jesus only, for the salvation of men in this world, than any other man that ever lived in it" (Doctrine and Covenants 135:3). It has also been said behind every great man is a great woman. Joseph Smith chose who his companion would be. In his own words she was the "choice of my heart." She fulfilled every request made of her by her husband. From the very moment Joseph went to the Hill Cumorah to obtain the gold plates, through the translation of the Book of Mormon, through every ordinance Joseph restored, from the creation of The Church of Jesus Christ of Latter-day Saints, through the trials and sufferings of persecution and all other vicissitudes of life, she stood by her husband; she remains an "Elect Lady." When Joseph was taken from her, she bore and surmounted trials that would have collapsed any other woman, and yet she raised her family with love, charity, and tenderness. In addition, she reached out and raised orphaned children and placed them under her protective wings. The scriptures teach that "charity is the pure love of Christ." Emma knew this principle and lived it.

We know of the contributions of Hyrum Smith, Samuel Smith, Oliver Cowdery, Brigham Young, David Whitmer, Sidney Rigdon, Martin Harris, and many, many others. Emma Hale Smith participated and contributed as much if not more than any other historical character in the history of The Church of Jesus Christ of Latter-day Saints. She has left a rich legacy for all mankind. Also, any person who has visited the historical sites in Nauvoo and felt of the Spirit there must credit her for the sacrifices she made to preserve that history. Anyone who has read the Joseph Smith Translation of the Bible must credit her for the sacrifice she made to preserve that record. Every woman who attends Relief Society should appreciate the foundation she built for them. Many of the songs that invite the Spirit into Church meetings remain to this day as a result of her efforts.

Emma is my grandmother, and I love her. I am proud to be part of her legacy. Joseph Smith, the head of this dispensation, has claimed Emma to be his eternal companion. They both have had their calling and election made sure. We have to be careful. Too often we judge history while Heavenly Father expects us to live by faith. We may resent it, appreciate it, respect it, honor it, but never judge it.

Where Are My Children?

Song written by Lorena Normandeau (1915–2004), great-granddaughter of Emma Smith. The song was sung by Emma's descendants at the family reunion in 2007.

Joseph, can it really be 35 years since you were taken from me?
Time seems to slip through my fingers. Days run into weeks and months into years.
Yet I am here; and Julia is here to comfort me.
Alexander and Joseph were here the other day asking questions about the past.
Till then I had managed to forget the bad and live for the good.
Now, my mind and heart flood with memories, bitter and sweet.
My heart is breaking again.
How long must I wait for those I love?
Joseph. Where are the tiny faces that we long to kiss?
Where is our newborn daughter, those lovely sons?
I wrote their names in our bible: Alvin, Thadeus, Louisa, my stillborn son, and our lost little Joseph.
Last night I saw you again. You were here. Whether a dream or a vision I do not know, but we stood together in the most beautiful mansion I ever saw.
I saw my precious Don Carlos.

What of David? What of Frederick? Will we be together
as we were promised?
Tell me Joseph. Tell me!
Where are the rest of my children?

Verse 1
(Joseph)
Be patient, Emma, for they await you;
Their lovely faces you shall behold.
The Lord has promised, and He is faithful;
All He has gathered, He shall restore.

(Emma)
My heart is empty and sick with longing,
And still I wait as the years unfold.
(Joseph)
Be patient, Emma, He will not fail you.
You'll have your children forevermore.

Verse 2
(Descendants)
Be patient, Mother, for we await you;
Our smiling faces you shall behold.
The Lord has promised, and He is faithful;
Your scattered children He shall restore.

Our hearts are tender; we yearn to know you,
And still we wait as the years unfold.
Be patient, Mother, we will not fail you.
We'll be together forevermore.[20]

We know Emma, Joseph, and all their children are united in heaven. Today, we as their posterity gather together here on earth to honor our Mother Emma and Father Joseph.

—Darcy Kennedy and Angeline Kennedy Washburn

Portraits of Emma Smith and Joseph Smith
from the Family Photo Album Collection.

Emma's Passing

Emma departed this life April 30, 1879, and on May 9, the Nauvoo Independent Newspaper carried the story of Emma's life, from her birth, to her marriage to Joseph Smith, through the births of her children and the many heart-rending trials she endured. Soon these descriptions gave way to seeing Emma through the eyes of those who surrounded and loved her.

As I read I couldn't help but see the similarities of Emma with one who lived long ago by the name of Tabitha. "Now there was at Joppa a certain disciple named Tabitha, which by interpretation is called Dorcas: this woman was full of good works and alms deeds which she did. And it came to pass in those days, that she was sick, and died; whom when they had washed, they laid her in an upper chamber." The disciples called for Peter and asked him not to delay his coming. "Then Peter arose and went with them. When he was come, they brought him into the upper chamber; and all the widows stood by him weeping, and showing the coats and garments which Dorcas made, while she was with them." (Acts 9:36-43)

This same kind of outpouring of love and affection greeted me as I continued to read of Emma in the Nauvoo Independent Newspaper: "She was loved and respected by all her neighbors, for her charitable and kind disposition. She was a good and faithful wife, a kind and loving mother, as the expressions of her children and associates will verify. If such a record as she has left does not render such a person worthy of a better life beyond, it is difficult to conceive how it can be done.

"The body of Mrs. Bidamon was laid in the parlor of the Mansion, where she resided, on the morning after her demise, and in the evening of the same day was placed in a burial case, where it was constantly watched by Mrs. Middleton (Julia Smith), the inmates of the Major's house, and a few intimate friends, until the afternoon of Friday, May 2. At twelve M., [sic] the friends and relatives of the deceased began to arrive, and at 2 p.m., the hour set for the services, the rooms were filled, and a large number in attendance who could not find entrance stood at the open doors to listen.

"After the services were over, the large company filed through the room past the coffin, viewing the face of the deceased as they passed. It was a touching sight to see those citizens so long acquainted with the silent sleeper while she was living, pause beside her to take a last look at the peaceful face, so calm amid the grief of the assembly. Now and then one to whom she had been dearer than to others, would caress the extended hand, or gently stooping lay a hand upon the cold face or forehead, some even kissing the pale cheek in an impulse of love and regret.

"The assembly was large. Almost every one knew Mrs. Bidamon, some intimately and for many years, some but for a few months; but it is safe to say the respect, esteem and love with which she was regarded by all, is but a just tribute to the sterling virtues of the woman, wife, and mother, whom the community so soberly, so sadly, and so tenderly laid away to rest on that beautiful May day, by the side of the Father of Waters, the mighty Mississippi."[21]

Appendix

Children of
Joseph Smith, Jr. and Emma Hale Smith

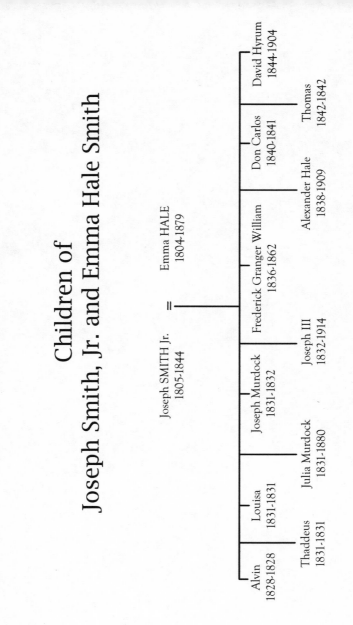

Joseph SMITH Jr. 1805-1844 = Emma HALE 1804-1879

Alvin 1828-1828

Thaddeus 1831-1831

Louisa 1831-1831

Julia Murdock 1831-1880

Joseph Murdock 1831-1832

Joseph III 1832-1914

Frederick Granger William 1836-1862

Alexander Hale 1838-1909

Don Carlos 1840-1841

Thomas 1842-1842

David Hyrum 1844-1904

Contributors to This Book

David J. Denning, Coral C. Smith Ambassador, The Joseph Smith Jr. and Emma Hale Smith Historical Society, Nebraska

Gracia Jones, Historian, The Joseph Smith Jr. and Emma Hale Smith Historical Society, Utah

Darcy Kennedy, Secretary, The Joseph Smith Jr. and Emma Hale Smith Historical Society, Utah

Michael A. Kennedy, Jr., United States and Australia Descendant Ambassador, The Joseph Smith Jr. and Emma Hale Smith Historical Society, Utah

Michael A. Kennedy, Sr., President, Joseph Smith Jr. and Emma Hale Smith Historical Society, Executive Producer of *Emma Smith–My Story*, Utah

Donna Smith Naegelin, Israel A. Smith Ambassador, The Joseph Smith Jr. and Emma Hale Smith Historical Society, Missouri

Lori Kay Savage, Coral C. Smith Ambassador, The Joseph Smith Jr. and Emma Hale Smith Historical Society, Montana

Tory Savage, Coral C. Smith Ambassador, The Joseph Smith Jr. and Emma Hale Smith Historical Society, Idaho

Dawn A. Schmith, Australia

Heather Smith Olivarez, Missouri

Kimberly Jo Smith, Arthur M. Smith Ambassador, The Joseph Smith Jr. and Emma Hale Smith Historical Society, Illinois

Nancy Sue Smith, Missouri

Robert Wendell Smith, Don A. Smith Ambassador, The Joseph Smith Jr. and Emma Hale Smith Historical Society, Nebraska

Shannon Smith, Missouri

Angeline Kennedy Washburn, Media Specialist, The Joseph Smith Jr. and Emma Hale Smith Historical Society, Utah

Notes

1.   Frederick Alexander Smith's Reminiscences, "Reflections of Emma" by Buddy Youngreen (1982): p. 115.

2.   Ibid., p. 67.

3.   Excerpts from a typed copy of the letter contained in: Kennedy, Emma Belle Smith, Original Journal, Courtesy Michael Kennedy, Sr.

4.   Kennedy, Emma Belle Smith, "Grandmother's Eyes," Original Journal, Courtesy Michael Kennedy, Sr.

5.   Jones, Gracia, "My Great-Great Grandmother," Ensign (August 1992), pp. 37–39.

6.   JSHC 5:107; Jones, Gracia, "Emma and Joseph: Their Divine Mission," (Covenant, 1999), p. 239.

7.   Original Minute Book, Courtesy of the Church Archives, The Church of Jesus Christ of Latter-day Saints.

8.   Kennedy, Emma Belle Smith, Original Journal, Courtesy Michael Kennedy, Sr. After Joseph's death, it was rumored there was a one thousand dollar ransom placed upon his head. Out of fear of his body being exhumed for this purpose, Joseph and Hyrum's bodies were not in the weighted caskets that were originally buried for public view. Their bodies were secretly buried in the dirt basement of the Nauvoo House. Around eight months later there were plans being made to do some work to the Nauvoo House, so in February 1845 Emma and Mary Fielding felt it was time for the reburial of Joseph and Hyrum. By the secrecy of night the bodies were moved about 75–100 feet from the Nauvoo House to the spring house by the old Homestead.

9.   Smith, Vida E., Biography of Alexander H. Smith, Independence, MO (2007).

10.   Kennedy, Emma Belle Smith, Original Journal, Courtesy Michael Kennedy, Sr.

11.   Ibid. 10.

12.   Ibid. 1, pp. 103–104

13.   The Vesta Pierce Crawford Collection, Ms 125, University of Utah Marriott Library.

14.   Smith, Vida E. "Ancestry and Posterity of Joseph Smith and Emma Hale," compiled by Mary Audentia Smith Anderson (Independence, Missouri: Herald Publishing House , 1929).

15.   Emma Josepha Smith McCallum, "Reflections of Emma" by Buddy Youngreen, pp. 59–60.

16.   Ibid. 1, p. 99

17.   Ibid. 11, p. 61

18.   Copy in author's possession, given by someone who had found the yellowed page in their great-grandmother's Bible.

19.   Excerpt from Smith, David, "An Appeal to My Brother Frederick," David Hyrum Smith, Poems, Accounts and Diary, 1853–64, pp. 25–26, David H. Smith Papers: Community of Christ Archives, Independence, MO. At the time of Joseph's death (June 27, 1844) Emma was carrying their 11th child, David, who would be born November 18, 1844.

20.   Normandeau, Lorena, "Where Are My Children?" courtesy of Gracia Jones.

21.   Excerpts from the Nauvoo Independent Newspaper (May 9, 1879).

The following are available for purchase at www.josephsmithjr.org.

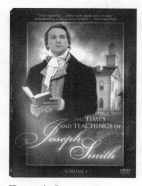

The Times and Teachings of Joseph Smith, Volume 1
A DVD of 14 film vignettes showing precious moments of the Prophet Joseph's life, his teachings, and his influence.

Emma's Letters
A collection of letters written between Emma and her children; letters to and from Governor Carlin, and more.

Emma's Quilt
This kit is based on the Emma Hale Smith Quilt on display in the Mansion House in Nauvoo, Illinois. It includes the pattern, directions and fabric for a 30 x 30 inch wall hanging top for 4 blocks of a quilt. Smith family oral history says that Emma used material from Joseph and Hyrum Smith's suits. The original quilt uses a variety of fabrics, and you can add the materials of your choice.

Proceeds from "The Times and Teachings of Joseph Smith" and "Emma's Letters" go to The Joseph Smith Jr. and Emma Hale Smith Historical Society. Proceeds from "Emma's Quilt" go to the preservation of the Emma, Joseph, and family grave site.